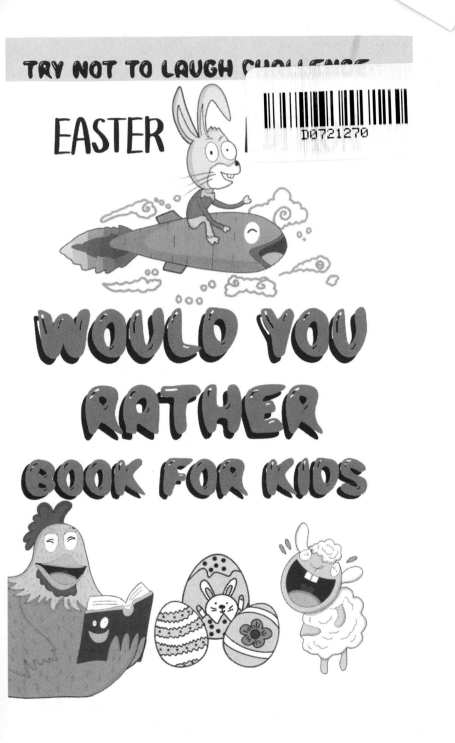

Would You Rather Book for Kids -Easter Edition- / Cutesaurs Press.
ISBN: 9798713054649

Welcome to Would you Rather

Book for Kids -Easter Edition-

Collect your freebies

Simply send us an email with the book title to:

Cutesauruspress@gmail.com

And you will get 10 pages

of Easter-themed funny jokes.

CUTESAURUS
PRESS

THANK YOU

We would like to personally thank you for

purchasing this book. If you have any

suggestions or requests, please don't

hesitate to contact us at:

cutesauruspress@gmail.com

YOUR VOICE MATTERS

we would be very grateful if you posted your

review on Amazon.

Share your feedback to help us improve and

benefit others from your experience.

Table of contents

Rules of the game

1- First of all, you need at least two players and have to decide who is 'Bunny 1'and who is 'Bunny 2'. If you have more than 2 players to play the game , you can decide which player belongs to 'Bunny group 1' and 'Bunny group 2'.

2- Sit across from each other and make eye contact.

3- The book consists of 8 rounds and starting with 'Bunny 1', read the would you rather question aloud and pick an answer. The same player will then explain why he/she chose that answer in the silliest and most hilarious way possible.

4- If the reason makes ' Bunny 2' laugh or even crack a smile, then 'Bunny 1' gets a point.

5- Take turns going back and forth , then mark your total laugh scores at the end of each round.

6- Whoever gets the most laugh scores is officially the " Laugh Master".

Egg-stra tip: Try to make funny voices, silly dance moves or wacky facial expressions to make your opponent crack up with laughter.

Remember: The scenarios listed in the book are for fun and games. please do not attempt any scenarios at home!

Egg-joy and have a Hoppy Easter!

Happy

Easter

Round

1

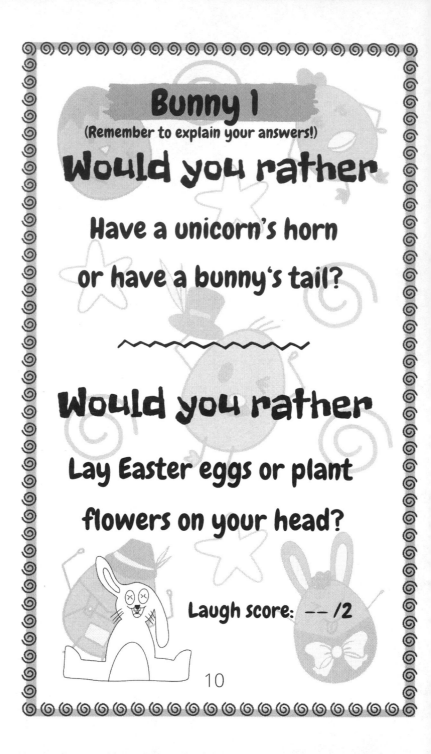

Bunny 1

Would you rather

Have a unicorn's horn

or have a bunny's tail?

~~~~~~

Would you rather

Lay Easter eggs or plant

flowers on your head?

Laugh score: –– /2

10

Bunny 2

Would you rather

Do the Chicken dance in front

of your classmates or do the

Macarena dance in front

of your classmates?

Would you rather

Have bunny ears or have

bunny whiskers?

Laugh score: —— /2

11

Bunny 1

(Remember to explain your answers!)

Would you rather

Paint your face like an Easter egg or decorate your hair like a Christmas tree?

~~~~~~~~

Would you rather

Be a giant with a rabbit's head or be a dwarf with a chicken's head?

Laugh score: −− /2

12

Bunny 2

Would you rather

Have springs on your feet that can help you hop like a rabbit or have stretchy ears that can help you reach things?

Would you rather

See an Easter egg come to life or see an Easter egg that can dance?

Laugh score: –– /2

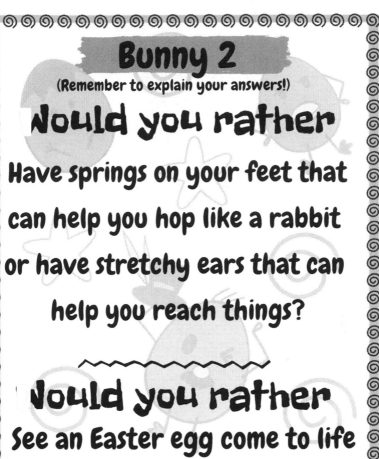

13

Bunny 1

(Remember to explain your answers!)

Would you rather

Have hedgehog's spines for hair or have rabbit's furry feet?

~~~~~~~~~~

Would you rather

Have buck teeth like a bunny or have no teeth like a bird?

Laugh score: -- /2

(Remember to explain your answers!)

Would you rather

Sleep in a chicken coop with 100 chickens or sleep in a cage with 10 monkeys?

~~~~~~~~

Would you rather

Lick a rabbit's nose or pick a pig's nose?

Laugh score: ―― /2

Add up your points and record them below.

Bunny 1 _____ / 6

Round total

Bunny 2 _____ / 6

Round total

Round Champion

_____

Round

2

Bunny 1

Would you rather

Pick up rabbits' poo with your mouth or feed baby birds worms with your mouth?

~~~~~~~~

Would you rather

Drink a cup of raw eggs or drink a bottle of sea water?

Laugh score: –– /2

18

Bunny 2

(Remember to explain your answers!)

Would you rather

Eat a salad made out of grass

or eat a pie filled with

flowers?

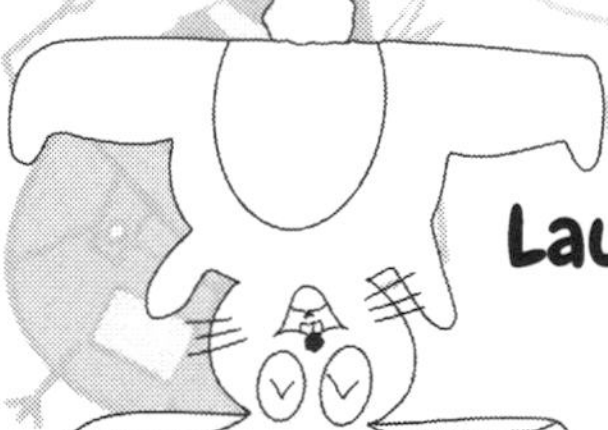

Would you rather

Touch rose thorns or touch

hedgehog spines?

Laugh score: -- /2

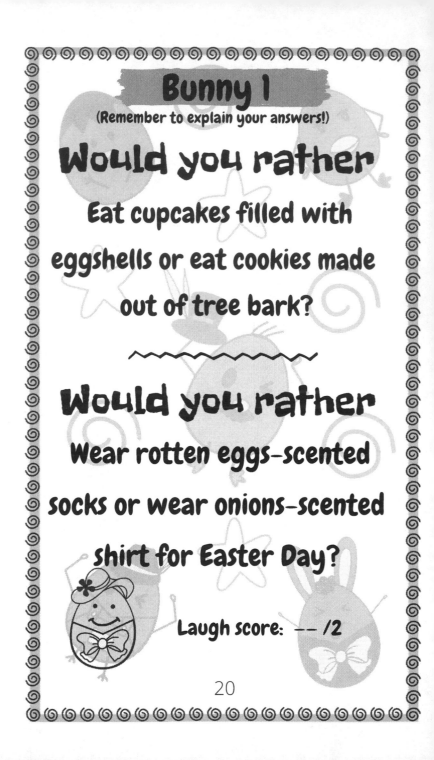

Bunny 1

(Remember to explain your answers!)

Would you rather

Eat cupcakes filled with eggshells or eat cookies made out of tree bark?

~~~~~~~~

Would you rather

Wear rotten eggs-scented socks or wear onions-scented shirt for Easter Day?

Laugh score: –– /2

Bunny 2

(Remember to explain your answers!)

Would you rather

Wear clothes made out of

grass or wear clothes made

out of bird feathers for

a week?

Would you rather

Have a butterfly's antenna

or have a bee' stinger?

Laugh score: —— /2

21

Bunny 1

Would you rather

Be a chick or be a duckling

for the rest of your life?

~~~~~~~~

Would you rather

Eat a chocolate easter bunny

filled with mayonnaise

or filled with ketchup?

Laugh score: –– /2

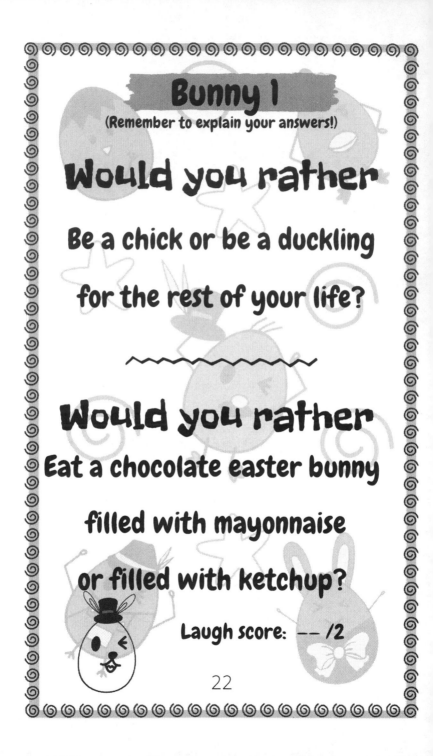

22

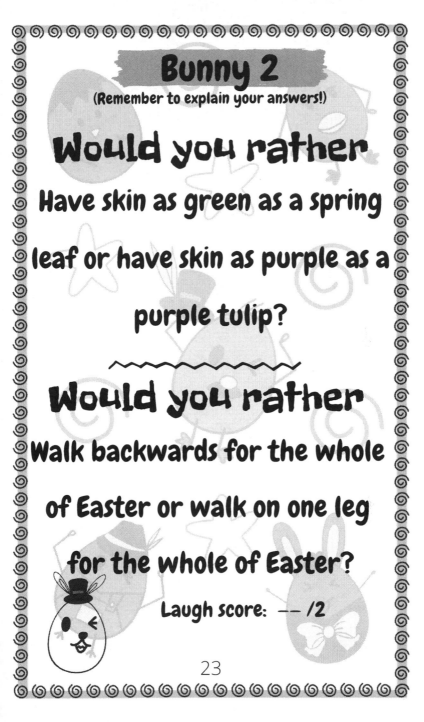

Bunny 2

(Remember to explain your answers!)

Would you rather

Have skin as green as a spring leaf or have skin as purple as a purple tulip?

〰〰〰

Would you rather

Walk backwards for the whole of Easter or walk on one leg for the whole of Easter?

Laugh score: —— /2

23

Add up your points and record them below.

Bunny 1 _____ / 6

Round total

Bunny 2 _____ / 6

Round total

Round Champion

_____

Round

3

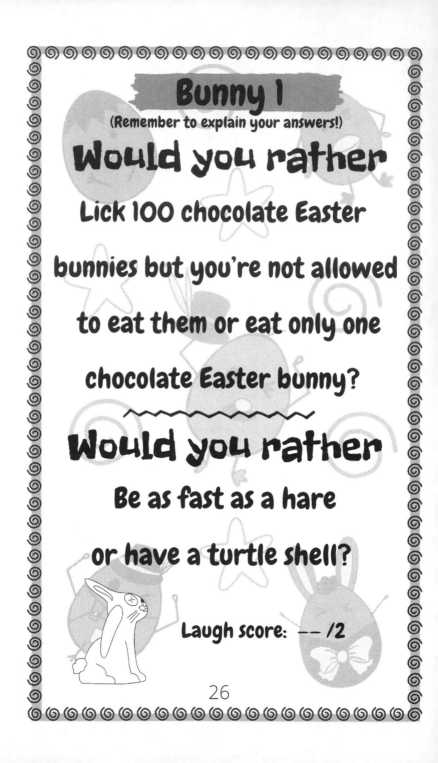

Bunny 1

(Remember to explain your answers!)

Would you rather

Lick 100 chocolate Easter

bunnies but you're not allowed

to eat them or eat only one

chocolate Easter bunny?

Would you rather

Be as fast as a hare

or have a turtle shell?

Laugh score: —— /2

26

Bunny 2

(Remember to explain your answers!)

Would you rather

Eat Easter cookies for 6 months

or eat jellybeans for 6 months?

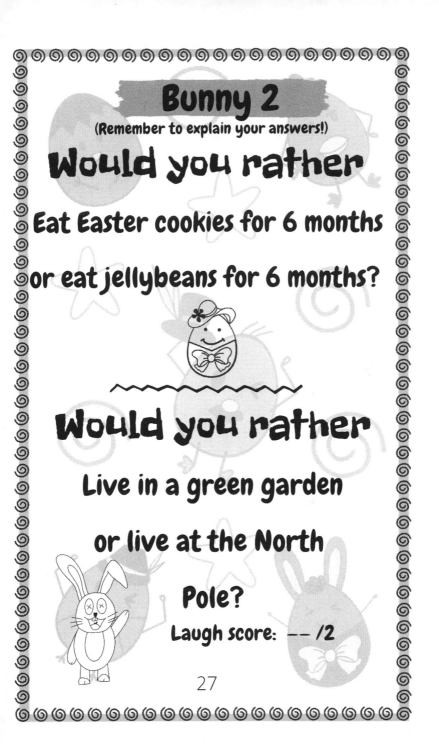

Would you rather

Live in a green garden

or live at the North

Pole?

Laugh score: –– /2

27

(Remember to explain your answers!)

Would you rather

Be part of an ant colony

or be part of a beehive?

~~~~~~

Would you rather

Live in a bird nest or live in

a rabbit burrow?

Laugh score: —— /2

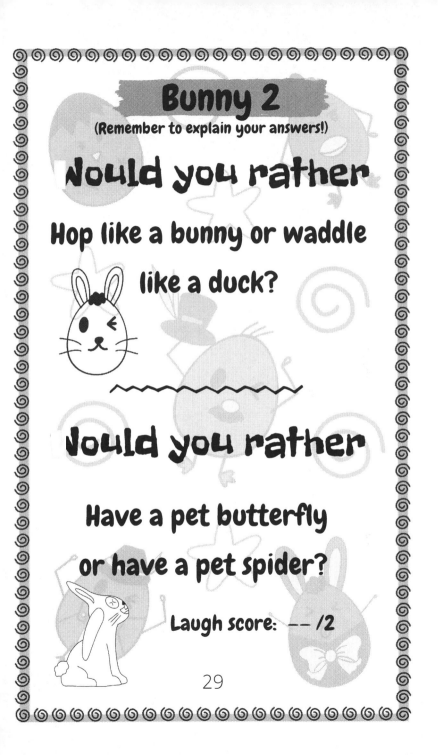

Bunny 2
(Remember to explain your answers!)

Would you rather

Hop like a bunny or waddle like a duck?

~~~~~~~~~~~~

Would you rather

Have a pet butterfly or have a pet spider?

Laugh score: –– /2

Bunny 1

(Remember to explain your answers!)

Would you rather

Be smart and get no Easter candies or be dumb and have a very big Easter basket filled with your favorite candies?

Would you rather

Get locked in a room with 10 bunnies for a day or get locked with one monkey for a week?

Laugh score: __ /2

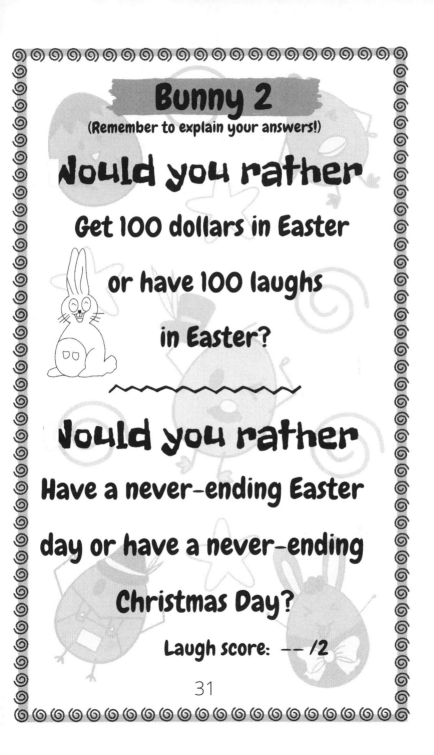

Would you rather

Get 100 dollars in Easter

or have 100 laughs

in Easter?

~~~~~~~~~~

Would you rather

Have a never-ending Easter

day or have a never-ending

Christmas Day?

Laugh score: —— /2

Add up your points and record them below.

Bunny 1 _____ / 6

Round total

Bunny 2 _____ / 6

Round total

Round Champion

_____

Round

4

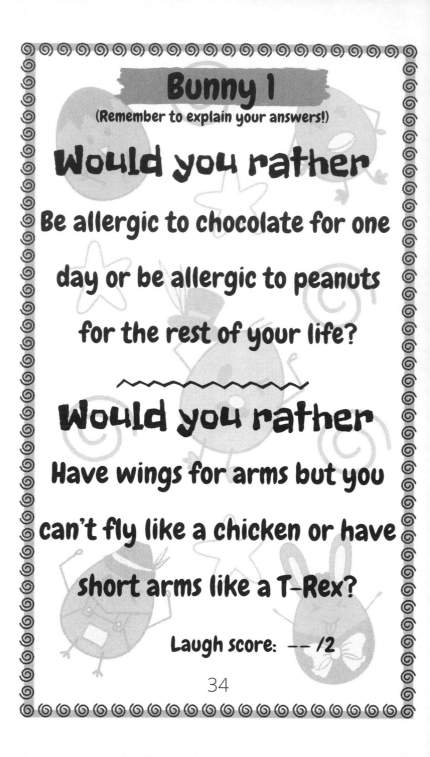

Bunny 1

(Remember to explain your answers!)

Would you rather

Be allergic to chocolate for one day or be allergic to peanuts for the rest of your life?

~~~~~~~

Would you rather

Have wings for arms but you can't fly like a chicken or have short arms like a T-Rex?

Laugh score: ‒‒ /2

Bunny 2

(Remember to explain your answers!)

Would you rather

Be unable to eat chocolate for one year or be unable to eat eggs for one year?

Would you rather

Be forced to listen to the same 5 Easter songs on repeat for one week or be forced to watch the same 5 Easter themed movies for one week?

Laugh score: —— /2

Bunny 1

(Remember to explain your answers!)

Would you rather

Discover a hidden treasure or find all the hidden Easter eggs?

~~~~~~~

Would you rather

Tweet like a bird after every sentence or baa like a sheep after every sentence?

Laugh score: —— /2

36

Bunny 2

Would you rather

Be a melting chocolate bunny

or be a melting

snowman?

Would you rather

Not to celebrate Easter or

not to celebrate

Christmas?

Laugh score: —— /2

37

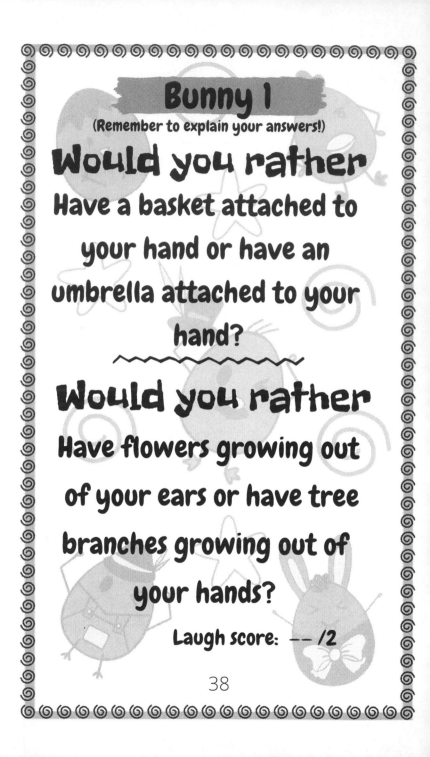

Bunny 1
(Remember to explain your answers!)

Would you rather

Have a basket attached to your hand or have an umbrella attached to your hand?

Would you rather

Have flowers growing out of your ears or have tree branches growing out of your hands?

Laugh score: –– /2

38

Bunny 2

(Remember to explain your answers!)

Would you rather

Paint 100 easter eggs

or eat 100 boiled

eggs?

~~~~~~~~~~

Would you rather

It rains jellybeans or it rains

Marshmallows?

Laugh score: __ /2

Add up your points and record them below.

/ 6

Bunny 1 _____

Round total

/ 6

Bunny 2 _____

Round total

Round Champion

_____

Round

5

Bunny 1

(Remember to explain your answers!)

Would you rather

Fly like a bird or jump like a

frog for the Easter

eggs hunt?

~~~~~~~~

Would you rather

Have wool like a lamb for hair

or have fur like a rabbit

for hair?

Laugh score: — — /2

42

Bunny 2

(Remember to explain your answers!)

Would you rather

Have grass for hair or have

an Easter egg for

a nose?

Would you rather

Wear a bunny costume or

wear a chicken costume

out in public?

Laugh score: —— /2

Bunny 1

Would you rather

Find an Easter egg full of candies or find an Easter egg full of money?

~~~~~~~~~~

Would you rather

Get a large Easter basket to share or a small Easter basket just for you?

Laugh score: —— /2

Bunny 2

(Remember to explain your answers!)

Would you rather

Have rainbow hair

or have rainbow

skin ?

Would you rather

Have bunny ears or have

a chicken beak?

Laugh score: —— /2

45

Bunny 1

(Remember to explain your answers!)

Would you rather

Eat bugs like a bird or eat grass like a lamb?

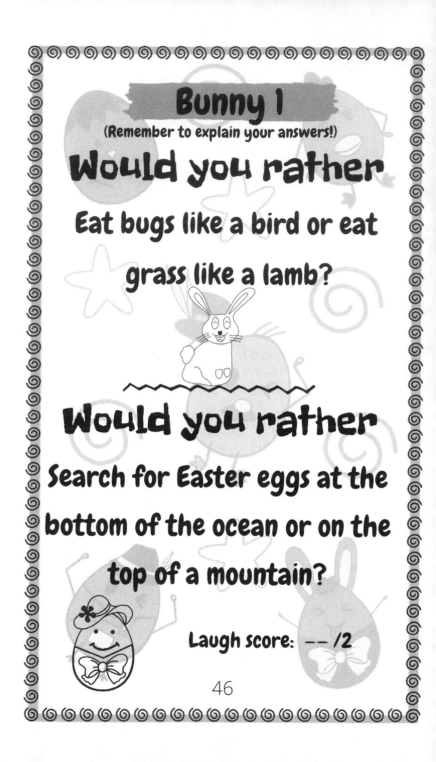

Would you rather

Search for Easter eggs at the bottom of the ocean or on the top of a mountain?

Laugh score: —— /2

46

(Remember to explain your answers!)

Would you rather

Eat carrots for a month or

eat hard-boiled eggs

for a month?

~~~~~~~~~~

Would you rather

Cluck like a chicken or squeak

like a rabbit?

Laugh score: —— /2

47

Add up your points and record them below.

Bunny 1 / 6

Round total

Bunny 2 / 6

Round total

Round Champion

Round

6

Bunny 1

Would you rather

Be a giant rabbit or be a tiny chicken?

Would you rather

Have a giant chocolate Easter egg or have a small golden egg?

Laugh score: ‑‑ /2

50

Bunny 2

(Remember to explain your answers!)

Would you rather

Go to a friend's house or go to

a park for an Easter

egg hunt?

~~~~~~~~~~

Would you rather

Hunt Easter eggs in the dark

or hunt Easter eggs in

the rain?

Laugh score: —— /2

51

Bunny 1

(Remember to explain your answers!)

Would you rather

Eat a giant chocolate bunny

 or eat a giant

jellybean?

Would you rather

Have a butterfly flying around

your head or have a chicken

setting on your head?

Laugh score: —— /2

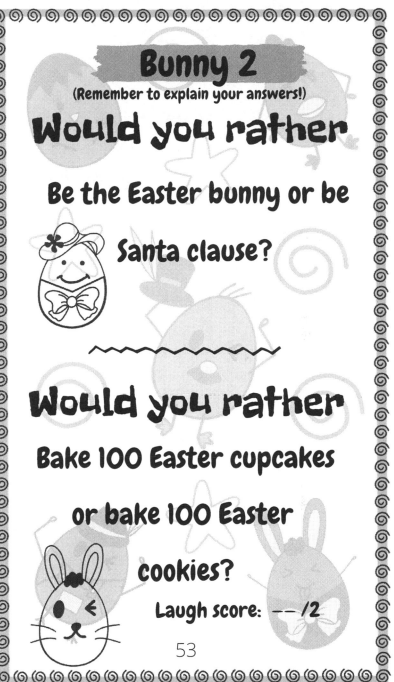

Bunny 2

(Remember to explain your answers!)

Would you rather

Be the Easter bunny or be Santa clause?

~~~~~~~~~~

Would you rather

Bake 100 Easter cupcakes or bake 100 Easter cookies?

Laugh score: __ /2

Bunny 1

(Remember to explain your answers!)

Would you rather

Roll down a cotton candy hill

or jump into a pit of

jelly beans?

~~~~~~~~~~

Would you rather

Find chocolate or find toys in

your Easter basket?

Laugh score: ―― /2

54

Bunny 2

(Remember to explain your answers!)

Would you rather

Ride the Easter bunny

or fly on a butterfly?

Would you rather

Attend an Easter parade or

go to an amusement park?

Laugh score: —— /2

55

Add up your points and record them below.

/6

Bunny 1 _____

Round total

/6

Bunny 2 _____

Round total

Round Champion

_____

Round

7

Bunny 1

Would you rather

Color Easter eggs or color an

Easter picture?

Would you rather

Spend a day with the Easter

bunny or spend a day with

Santa Claus?

Laugh score: __ /2

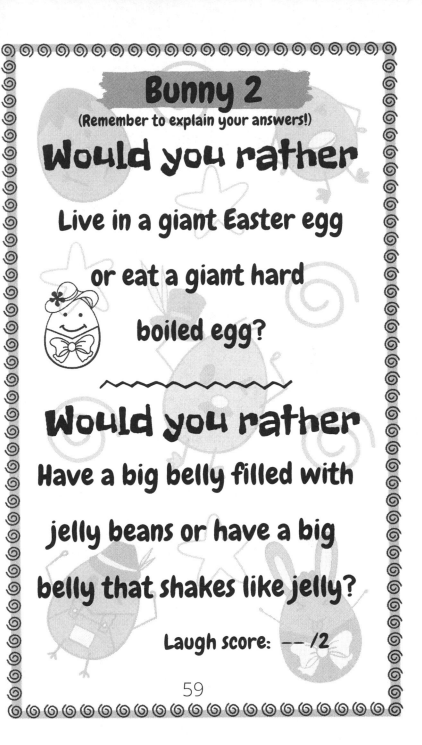

Bunny 2

(Remember to explain your answers!)

Would you rather

Live in a giant Easter egg

or eat a giant hard

boiled egg?

Would you rather

Have a big belly filled with

jelly beans or have a big

belly that shakes like jelly?

Laugh score: —— /2

59

Bunny 1

(Remember to explain your answers!)

Would you rather

Have the power to find all the hidden Easter eggs in one minute or color 100 Easter eggs in one minute?

~~~~~~~~~

Would you rather

Eat only boiled eggs all April or eat only Broccoli all April?

Laugh score: —— /2

Bunny 2

(Remember to explain your answers!)

Would you rather

Eat chocolate Easter bunny with the Easter bunny or bake Easter cookies with the Easter bunny?

Would you rather

Wear a bunny costume or wear a butterfly costume to school everday?

Laugh score: –– /2

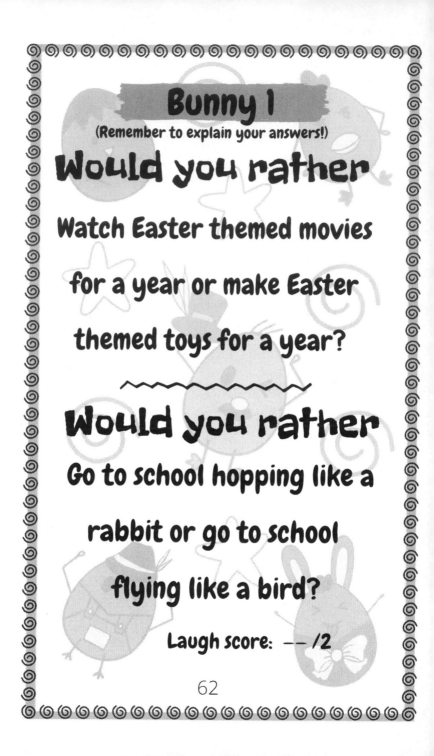

Bunny 1

(Remember to explain your answers!)

Would you rather

Watch Easter themed movies

for a year or make Easter

themed toys for a year?

Would you rather

Go to school hopping like a

rabbit or go to school

flying like a bird?

Laugh score: —— /2

62

Bunny 2

Would you rather

Have a small piece of roast lamb for Easter dinner or have a big piece of burnt ham for Easter dinner?

Would you rather

Be a bunny and receive a giant carrot for Easter or be a cat and receive a giant fish for Easter?

Laugh score: ── /2

Add up your points and record them below.

Bunny 1

/ 6

_____

Round total

Bunny 2

/ 6

_____

Round total

Round Champion

_____

Round

8

Bunny 1

Would you rather

Not to celebrate Easter every year or not to celebrate your birthday every year?

Would you rather

Receive one big Easter baskets or receive 10 small Easter baskets?

Laugh score: —— /2

66

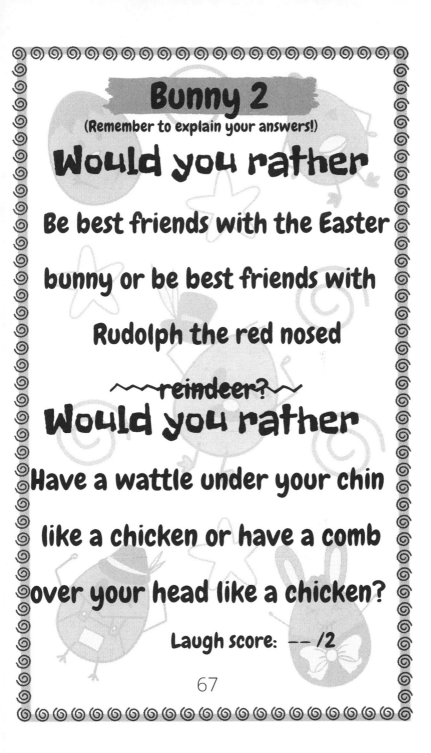

Bunny 2

(Remember to explain your answers!)

Would you rather

Be best friends with the Easter

bunny or be best friends with

Rudolph the red nosed

~~reindeer?~~

Would you rather

Have a wattle under your chin

like a chicken or have a comb

over your head like a chicken?

Laugh score: –– /2

Bunny 1

(Remember to explain your answers!)

Would you rather

Have bunny's teeth or have

monkey's ears?

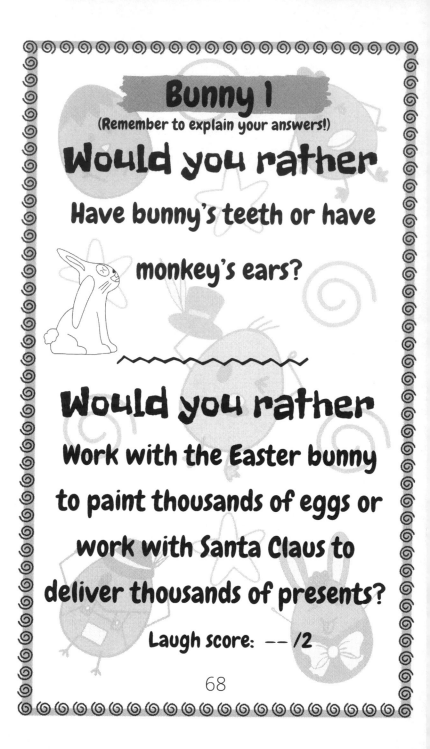

Would you rather

Work with the Easter bunny to paint thousands of eggs or work with Santa Claus to deliver thousands of presents?

Laugh score: —— /2

68

Would you rather

Go on an Easter hunt in a muddy field or go on an Easter hunt in a haunted house?

Would you rather

Have long ears like a rabbit or have sharp claws like a tiger ?

Laugh score: –– /2

Bunny 1

Would you rather

smell like a chicken or smell

like a skunk?

~~~~~~~~~~

Would you rather

Have candy canes for fingers

or have jellybeans for eyes?

Laugh score: —— /2

Bunny 2

(Remember to explain your answers!)

Would you rather

Live without candies or live

without eggs?

Would you rather

Be Peter Rabbit or be Zeus

from the movie 'The Dog

Who Saved Easter'?

Laugh score: —— /2

Add up your points and record them below.

Bunny 1

/6
_____
Round total

Bunny 2

/6
_____
Round total

Round Champion

_____

Add up your points and record them below.

Bunny 1

/ 48
_____
Game total

Bunny 2

/ 48
_____
Game total

Laugh Master

_____

THANK YOU
We hope you
Egg-joy it!

Made in the USA
Columbia, SC
08 March 2023